TEN NOSEY WEKA

For Ava, Henry and all the other tchimirik' (children) of Rēkohu.

Ta rē Moriori is the language of the Moriori, the first people to live on Rēkohu/Chatham Island and Rangihaute/Pitt Island. It shares similarities with te reo Māori, but is a language in its own right.

This book has been produced in consultation with the Hokotehi Moriori Trust, the organisation that represents the Moriori people.

With thanks to Justin Kereama for proofing te reo Māori in the book.

Each page includes a number and word to learn as you read in Moriori, Māori and English. There is a glossary at the back of the book to review all the words and numbers that you have learned as you read about these nosey weka.

TEN NOSEY WEKA

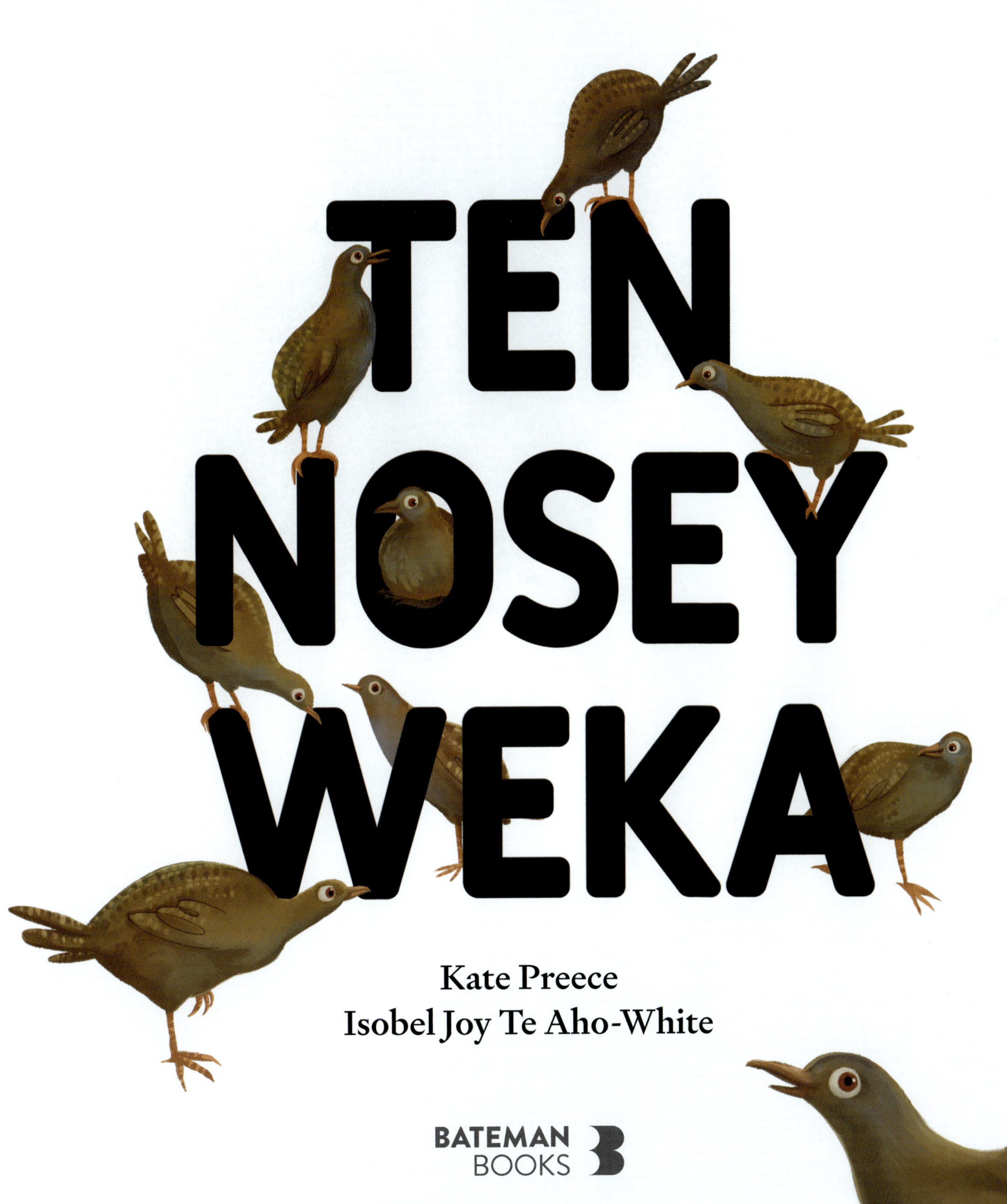

Kate Preece
Isobel Joy Te Aho-White

BATEMAN BOOKS

10

Tengahuru / tekau / ten

Ten nosey weka
Scurried in a line.
One ran to the roto
Then there were . . .

roto
roto
lake

9

Teiwa / iwa / nine

Nine nosey weka
Squeezed under a gate.
One hid in harapepe
Then there were . . .

harapepe

harakeke

flax

8

Tewaru / waru / eight

Eight nosey weka
Had a food obsession.
One tasted tupere
Then there were . . .

tupere
tuangi
cockles

7

Tewhitu / whitu / seven

Seven nosey weka
Scratched among the sticks.
One nibbled ngarara
Then there were . . .

ngarara
ngārara
insects

6

Teono / ono / six

Six nosey weka
Were lucky to survive.
One mocked a mimiha
Then there were . . .

mimiha

kekeno

seal

5

Terima / rima / five

Five nosey weka
Pecked along the shore.
One wrestled rimu
Then there were . . .

rimu
rimurimu
seaweed

4

Tewha / whā / four

Four nosey weka
Passed a kōpi tree.
One pecked a purehe
Then there were . . .

purehe
pūngāwere
spider

3

Toru / toru / three

Three nosey weka
Had a lovely view.
One touched the taheke
Then there were . . .

taheke
tāheke
waterfall

2

Teru / rua / two

Two nosey weka
Looked about for fun.
One teased a tchuna
Then there was . . .

tchuna
tuna
eel

1

Tehi / tahi / one

One nosey weka
Was a hungry hen.
When she gnawed on ngana
Then there were . . .

Moriori were the first people to live on Rēkohu/ Chatham Island and Rangihaute/Pitt Island. Their language is called ta rē Moriori.

Ta rē Moriori is one of 38 Polynesian languages. It is most closely related to Māori, Rarotongan, Tahitian and Hawaiian. Often compared to te reo Māori, the two languages have similar pronunciations, but different alphabets, and ta rē Moriori has unique words and rules, too.

Thousands of people around the world have Moriori karāpuna/ancestors. By learning ta rē Moriori, we discover more about an important part of New Zealand's history and keep the language alive for generations to come.

Counting Game

Weka has lots of different friends on the island — did you spot them as you read? See how many of each creature you can find throughout the story. Can you say your answer in ta rē Moriori and te reo Māori?

Answers on last page

Glossary

Ta rē Moriori	Te reo Māori	English
roto	roto	lake
harapepe	harakeke	flax
tupere	tuangi	cockles
ngarara	ngārara	insects
mimiha	kekeno	seal
rimu	rimurimu	seaweed
purehe	pūngāwere	spider
taheke	tāheke	waterfall
tchuna	tuna	eel
ngana	hua	fruit
tehi	tahi	one
teru	rua	two
toru	toru	three
tewha	whā	four
terima	rima	five
teono	ono	six
tewhitu	whitu	seven
tewaru	waru	eight
teiwa	iwa	nine
tengahuru	tekau	ten

10 Weka Facts!

Tehi (tahi) –
Weka can't fly, but they can run very quickly!

Teru (rua) –
A weka nest is shaped like a cup and made from grass and leaves, tucked away in a small space.

Toru (toru) –
Weka are omnivores, which means they eat meat, fruit, insects, vegetables and plants.

Tewha (whā) –
Weka are known for their curious nature and will be very brave if there is food around.

Terima (rima) –
The lightest weka weighs about the same as a block of butter, but the heaviest can be as heavy as a big bag of sugar (1.5kg).

Teono (ono) –
Weka have excellent homing instincts and will cross land and sea to get back home.

Tewhitu (whitu) –
Tens of thousands of buff weka live on Rēkohu, where the bird can also be served up on the dinner table!

Tewaru (waru) –
Weka eggs are cream with purple-brown spots. A hen will lay up to tewha eggs in her nest.

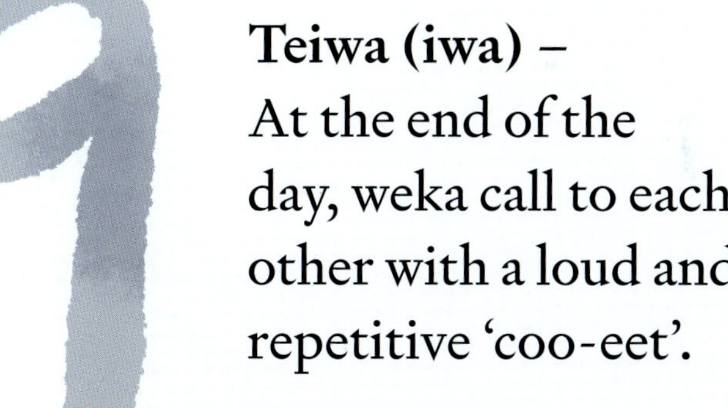

Teiwa (iwa) –
At the end of the day, weka call to each other with a loud and repetitive 'coo-eet'.

Tengahuru (tekau) –
Weka are only found in New Zealand, with different types living in different areas. The tewha subspecies are the North Island weka, western weka, buff weka, and Stewart Island weka.

Published in 2024 by David Bateman Ltd,
Unit 2/5 Workspace Drive, Hobsonville,
Auckland 0618, New Zealand
www.batemanbooks.co.nz
ISBN: 978-1-77689-104-7

Reprinted 2024.

A catalogue record for this book is available from the National Library of New Zealand.

Book design: Spencer Levine
Printed in China by Toppan Leefung Printing Ltd

Counting Game answers

10 sheep; 9 Chatham Island red admiral butterflies; 8 Chatham Island blue penguins; 7 Chatham Island mollymawks; 6 cows; 5 Chatham Island shags; 4 Chatham Island oystercatchers; 3 crayfish; 2 black swans; 1 pukeko